SCHIZOPHRENIA

NESSES AND DISORDERS
ss and Understanding

SCHIZOPHRENIA

H.W. Poole

SERIES CONSULTANT
ANNE S. WALTERS, PhD
Chief Psychologist, Emma Pendleton Bradley Hospital
Clinical Associate Professor, Alpert Medical School/Brown University

MASON CREST

Mason Crest
450 Parkway Drive, Suite D
Broomall, PA 19008
www.masoncrest.com

MTM Publishing, Inc.
435 West 23rd Street, #8C
New York, NY 10011
www.mtmpublishing.com

President: Valerie Tomaselli
Vice President, Book Development: Hilary Poole
Designer: Annemarie Redmond
Copyeditor: Peter Jaskowiak
Editorial Assistant: Andrea St. Aubin

Series ISBN: 978-1-4222-3364-1
ISBN: 978-1-4222-3375-7
Ebook ISBN: 978-1-4222-8576-3

Library of Congress Cataloging-in-Publication Data
Poole, Hilary W., author.
  Schizophrenia / by H.W. Poole.
      pages cm. — (Mental illnesses and disorders : awareness and understanding)
  Includes bibliographical references and index.
  ISBN 978-1-4222-3375-7 (hardback) — ISBN 978-1-4222-3364-1 (series) — ISBN
978-1-4222-8576-3 (ebook)
  1. Schizophrenia—Juvenile literature. I. Title.
  RC514.P655 2016
  616.89'8—dc23
                                                              2015006706

Printed and bound in the United States of America.

9 8 7 6 5 4 3 2

TABLE OF CONTENTS

Key Icons to Look for:

Words to Understand: These words with their easy-to-understand definitions will increase the reader's understanding of the text, while building vocabulary skills.

Sidebars: This boxed material within the main text allows readers to build knowledge, gain insights, explore possibilities, and broaden their perspectives by weaving together additional information to provide realistic and holistic perspectives.

Research Projects: Readers are pointed toward areas of further inquiry connected to each chapter. Suggestions are provided for projects that encourage deeper research and analysis.

Text-Dependent Questions: These questions send the reader back to the text for more careful attention to the evidence presented there.

Series Glossary of Key Terms: This back-of-the-book glossary contains terminology used throughout the series. Words found here increase the reader's ability to read and comprehend higher-level books and articles in this field.

People who cope with mental illnesses and disorders deserve our empathy and respect.

(istockphoto/digitalskillet)

Introduction to the Series

According to the National Institute of Mental Health, in 2012 there were an estimated 45 million people in the United States suffering from mental illness, or 19 percent of all US adults. A separate 2011 study found that among children, almost one in five suffer from some form of mental illness or disorder. The nature and level of impairment varies widely. For example, children and adults with anxiety disorders may struggle with a range of symptoms, from a constant state of worry about both real and imagined events to a complete inability to leave the house. Children or adults with schizophrenia might experience periods when the illness is well controlled by medication and therapies, but there may also be times when they must spend time in a hospital for their own safety and the safety of others. For every person with mental illness who makes the news, there are many more who do not, and these are the people that we must learn more about and help to feel accepted, and even welcomed, in this world of diversity.

It is not easy to have a mental illness in this country. Access to mental health services remains a significant issue. Many states and some private insurers have "opted out" of providing sufficient coverage for mental health treatment. This translates to limits on the amount of sessions or frequency of treatment, inadequate rates for providers, and other problems that make it difficult for people to get the care they need.

Meanwhile, stigma about mental illness remains widespread. There are still whispers about "bad parenting," or "the other side of the tracks." The whisperers imply that mental illness is something you bring upon yourself, or something that someone does to you. Obviously, mental illness can be exacerbated by an adverse event such as trauma or parental instability. But there is just as much truth to the biological bases of mental illness. No one is made schizophrenic by ineffective parenting, for example, or by engaging in "wild" behavior as an adolescent. Mental illness is a complex interplay of genes, biology, and the environment, much like many physical illnesses.

People with mental illness are brave soldiers, really. They fight their illness every day, in all of the settings of their lives. When people with an anxiety disorder graduate from college, you know that they worked very hard to get there—harder, perhaps, than those who did not struggle with a psychiatric issue. They got up every day with a pit in their stomach about facing the world, and they worried about their finals more than their classmates. When they had to give a presentation in class, they thought their world was going to end and that they would faint, or worse, in front of everyone. But they fought back, and they kept going. Every day. That's bravery, and that is to be respected and congratulated.

These books were written to help young people get the facts about mental illness. Facts go a long way to dispel stigma. Knowing the facts gives students the opportunity to help others to know and understand. If your student lives with someone with mental illness, these books can help students know a bit more about what to expect. If they are concerned about someone, or even about themselves, these books are meant to provide some answers and a place to start.

The topics covered in this series are those that seem most relevant for middle schoolers—disorders that they are most likely to come into contact with or to be curious about. Schizophrenia is a rare illness, but it is an illness with many misconceptions and inaccurate portrayals in media. Anxiety and depressive disorders, on the other hand, are quite common. Most of our youth have likely had personal experience of anxiety or depression, or knowledge of someone who struggles with these symptoms.

As a teacher or a librarian, thank you for taking part in dispelling myths and bringing facts to your children and students. Thank you for caring about the brave soldiers who live and work with mental illness. These reference books are for all of them, and also for those of us who have the good fortune to work with and know them.

—Anne S. Walters, PhD
Chief Psychologist, Emma Pendleton Bradley Hospital
Clinical Professor, Alpert Medical School/Brown University

CHAPTER ONE

UNDERSTANDING SCHIZOPHRENIA

Words to Understand

perception: awareness or understanding of reality.

schizophrenia: a severe mental disorder that involves a break between a person's understanding of reality and what is actually happening.

stereotype: a simplified idea about a type of person, not connected to actual individuals.

The disorder called **schizophrenia** has probably been around as long as humans have. But it has taken humans a very long time to understand it. Even today, there is a lot we don't know for sure.

"Madness" in History

Long ago, all types of mental disorders were lumped together as "madness" or "insanity." People believed that madness was a punishment from the gods. Some people thought that the person's mind had been taken over by a demon. For example, the Bible refers to an "evil spirit" that takes over the mind of Saul.

Most people viewed insanity as a curse. They thought a "mad" person must be bad or broken in some way. Some towns kept mentally ill people in a special building called the

A stained glass window in a cathedral in Brussels shows the Biblical figure Saul, later known as Saint Paul.

CURSE OR GIFT?

Even in ancient times, not everyone believed that madness was a curse. The Greek philosopher named Socrates supposedly said,

Madness . . . is the channel by which we receive the greatest blessings. . . . Madness is a finer thing than sober sense . . . madness comes from God, whereas sober sense is merely human.

Sophocles was saying that "insane" people have special insights the rest of us can't understand. This idea can still be found in books and movies today, where the "crazy" character is the also the wisest. But this **stereotype** is not very helpful to people with mental disorders. They are not better or worse than other people. They are human beings, just like everyone else.

"fool's tower." It's possible that some of the people who were burned as witches in colonial America were mentally ill.

Today we know that there is no catch-all category of "madness." Instead, there are many specific kinds of mental disorders. These disorders aren't curses, and they don't come from the sky. Mental disorders do not make you a bad person. And they are nobody's fault.

What Is Schizophrenia?

What we now call **schizophrenia** was described in the 1800s by Dr. Emil Kraepelin. He called the condition "dementia

SPLIT ISN'T MULTIPLE

Because the word schizophrenia means "split mind," people often confuse that disorder with a different one. The other illness is dissociative identity disorder (DID). It used to be called "multiple personality disorder."

People with DID have two or more personalities inside them. These personalities are called *alters*. One person can have as many as 100 different alters, although having about 10 is more common. Different alters don't just have different names. They are completely different people. Amazingly, some alters have different allergies or need different eyeglasses, even though the person's body stays the same.

We do not know exactly what causes DID. Sometimes the disorder is caused by a very traumatic experience, but not always. People who make films and television programs like to show people with DID because they seem "strange" to outsiders. But in truth, the disorder is very, very rare. As few as one-tenth of 1 percent of Americans may have it.

DID has no connection to schizophrenia. The "split" in schizophrenia refers to the split between the person's **perceptions** and the real world. Having schizophrenia might make you a sadder person or an angrier person, but it does not make you a different person.

praecox." He thought the symptoms came from a gradual decline of the brain.

In the early 1900s, Dr. Eugen Bleuler agreed with some of Kraepelin's ideas but disagreed with others. Where Kraeplin saw a decline, Bleuler saw a break from reality. He used the Greek words *skhizein* (split) and *phren* (mind) to create the term we use today.

Ever since Bleuler named the disorder, doctors have been trying to figure out why it occurs. There is probably no single factor that causes schizophrenia. Instead, a number of factors probably combine to cause the disorder. (Chapter two will discuss possible causes in more detail.)

What Is Going Wrong?

Everything you see, hear, and feel is sorted and understood by your brain. If you hear a chirping noise, you understand that a bird is outside your window. You don't need to actually see the bird, but you know that the bird is there. That's because your brain recognizes patterns: You've heard chirping birds before, and this sound is like those other sounds.

Or let's say you are in class. Your teacher speaks, and you hear the words she says. You understand from what you hear

Many people with schizophrenia hear threatening noises or voices.

WHAT DOES SCHIZOPHRENIA FEEL LIKE?

Some people say that schizophrenia feels like there is a radio in your head with loud, often hateful, sounds coming out. You can't turn this radio off, and you can't change the channel. You just have to get through the day, doing the things everyone else does, but with this annoying noise that you can't control. Author Elyn Sacks described her schizophrenia as a "waking nightmare."

that it is time to open your history book. A picture in the book reminds you of something funny your friend said, and you smile at the memory. But then you read about something terrible that happened, and it makes you frown.

Your brain interprets information so quickly that you don't even realize it. Sounds outside yourself, like the bird or your teacher, are separated from the sound of your own breathing. Something happening right now is separated from a memory of what your friend said. When you read something sad, you react in a sad way.

The brain of someone with schizophrenia is not able to sort all this information so easily. Someone with schizophrenia might think the bird is trying to give her a message. She might laugh at terrible news. But that's not because she thinks the news is funny. It's because her brain signals got mixed up.

Schizophrenia can be frightening for the person who is having these experiences, and it can also be frightening for the friends and families of people who are ill. In later chapters, we will talk about how the illness is treated, and also give you some tips for helping a friend or family member who has the disorder.

Text-Dependent Questions

1. What did people used to believe about mental illness, and what do we now know?
2. Where does the term *schizophrenia* come from?
3. What is going wrong in the brain of a person with schizophrenia?
4. What is the difference between schizophrenia and DID?

Research Project

According to the World Health Organisation, there are about 24 million people with schizophrenia in the world. Research schizophrenia rates in different countries, including developed versus developing nations.

CHAPTER TWO

CAUSES OF SCHIZOPHRENIA

Words to Understand

chronic: ongoing or returning again and again.

dopamine: a substance in the human body that helps transmit messages in the brain.

heredity: the passing of a trait from parents to children.

logical: reasonable; making sense.

serotonin: a chemical in the body that is involved in many vital functions, including appetite, memory, sleep, and body temperature.

If you have a broken arm, chances are you know why. If you have the flu, you might not know exactly *how* you caught it, but you know that a virus was involved. But the same is not true of schizophrenia. Its causes are difficult to explain.

Why Does It Happen?

As mentioned in chapter one, ancient people believed that the mentally ill were cursed or possessed. Later, people blamed an imbalance in "humours," which is an old term for bodily substances that people once believed controlled our health.

In the early 20th century, the famous doctor Sigmund Freud argued that bad parents (especially mothers) caused schizophrenia. This theory hurt a lot of people. Parents feel

Dr. Sigmund Freud was a very influential doctor who said schizophrenia was caused by bad parenting. We now know this is not true.

terrible when their child has a mental disorder. Making them feel guilty just makes the situation worse.

Doctors now know that good parents can still have sick children. And while the mystery of schizophrenia has not been solved, doctors do have some more **logical** theories.

Heredity and Environment

One possible cause is **heredity**. A person with two blue-eyed parents is likely to also have blue eyes. In the same way, a person with a schizophrenic in his family is more likely to have the disorder.

But heredity isn't the only answer. If it were, then identical twins would both have schizophrenia. But we know this is not always the case. If one twin has schizophrenia, the other has a

One way scientists learn more about mental disorders like schizophrenia is by studying twins.

CASE STUDY: MICHAEL

Michael was shy and lonely as a child. Other kids picked on him because he seemed "weird." Sometimes he would do unusual things, like staring at pictures of plants for hours.

Michael had more problems in high school. He would get very angry or even push other students for no reason. Sometimes he would laugh out loud at nothing. He talked to imaginary friends, but he made little sense when he talked to real people. He often talked about TV shows he watched as though they were real.

Michael's parents loved him even though he could be difficult. They took him to see many doctors over the years. He was diagnosed with **chronic** schizophrenia. He now takes a number of different medications to help manage his symptoms.

50 to 60 percent chance of also developing the disorder. That is a high percentage, but it is far from certain.

A person's surroundings may be another cause. It is possible that if a developing baby is exposed to certain viruses or poisons, that might contribute to schizophrenia. Lack of nutrition in the womb is another possible factor.

Brain Structure and Chemistry

The structure and chemistry of the brain itself might be another cause. In people with schizophrenia, researchers have found small differences in the size of certain areas of the brain compared to other people.

One brain chemical, called **dopamine**, is a top suspect in this mystery. Too much dopamine in one part of the brain is believed to cause some symptoms of schizophrenia.

Scientists are still trying to figure out the exact causes of schizophrenia. But the brain chemicals called serotonin and dopamine are prime suspects.

Interestingly, too *little* dopamine in another part of the brain may cause other symptoms.

The chemical **serotonin** may also play a role in schizophrenia. Serotonin is more often linked to mood disorders such as depression. But many doctors suspect that it has a role to play in schizophrenia, too.

There is still a lot we don't know. One thing we can say more definitely is who tends to develop schizophrenia. So, let's set aside the question of *why* and look at the question of *who*.

Who Develops the Disorder?

About 1 percent of the US population has schizophrenia. That sounds like a small number, but since the United States has more than 313 million people, even 1 percent is still a lot. The disorder also occurs in many other countries, both rich and poor ones.

Both men and women can develop the disorder. But in males, symptoms tend to appear in the late teens and early 20s. In females, the symptoms tend to show up a bit later—in the late 20s. People over the age of 40 almost never suddenly develop schizophrenia.

People once believed that younger kids could not have the disorder. But in fact doctors do see cases of younger

THE BRAIN BANK

When Dr. E. Fuller Torrey was in college, his sister developed schizophrenia. The doctors said that her illness was caused by the death of Fuller and Rhoda's father many years earlier. But this made no sense to Fuller. If the death of a parent caused schizophrenia, then why didn't Fuller have it also?

He decided to become a doctor himself. In time, Fuller became a top expert on schizophrenia. His book, *Surviving Schizophrenia: A Family Manual* (1983), is a great resource for people dealing with the illness.

In 1994, Dr. Torrey founded a brain bank. The bank collects the brains of mentally ill people after they die. The brains are frozen and sliced thin. The slices are shared with researchers all over the world. Scientists study the brains to learn more about the causes of mental illness. Dr. Torrey believes that the best way to find cures is for scientists to share information with each other. The brain bank helps make this possible.

people with the illness. Experts use names like "juvenile schizophrenia," "early-onset schizophrenia," or "childhood schizophrenia." The disorder is rare, but it does happen. Symptoms of schizophrenia in children are the same as those in adults. But sometimes kids with the disorder have been mistakenly diagnosed as autistic, because the symptoms can look similar.

It is more common for symptoms to show up in the teen years. Unfortunately, it can be difficult to diagnose schizophrenia in teenagers. Some of the symptoms can look like regular teenage behavior. The next chapter will talk about what those symptoms are, and why they are more than just "teenage blues."

DID YOU KNOW?

According to the World Health Organisation, about 50 percent of people with schizophrenia are not receiving the correct treatment. Of those people, about 90 percent live in developing countries.

Text-Dependent Questions

1. What are some of the old theories of schizophrenia that we now know are incorrect?
2. What do identical twins teach us about schizophrenia?
3. When is schizophrenia most likely to appear in boys? In girls?

Research Project

Find out more about brain chemistry. Why are substances like dopamine and serotonin so important to mental health?

SYMPTOMS OF SCHIZOPHRENIA

Words to Understand

affect: as a noun, the way someone seems on the outside—including attitude, emotion, and voice (pronounced with the emphasis on the first syllable, "AFF-eckt").

auditory: having to do with hearing or sound.

delusion: a false belief with no connection to reality.

hallucination: something a person sees or hears that is not really there.

olfactory: having to do with the sense of smell.

spectrum: a range; in medicine, from less extreme to more extreme.

tactile: having to do with the sense of touch.

Schizophrenia symptoms come in two types: positive and negative. Usually, when you hear the word *positive*, it usually means something good. The word *negative* tends to mean something bad. But when it comes to symptoms, doctors do not mean good or bad. The words *positive* and *negative* are not a judgment. Instead, the terms refer to the presence or absence of certain behaviors.

Positive Symptoms

People with schizophrenia have some experiences that healthy people don't. These are called positive symptoms. That doesn't mean the symptoms are good—it just means they exist in people who have the disorder but not in people who don't.

Delusions. A person with a **delusion** might believe he is something he isn't (for example, the president). Or he might believe something is true that isn't (for example, that he can fly). One common delusion is that someone or something is trying to control the person's mind. It is nearly impossible to talk a person out of his delusions.

Hallucinations. Some people with schizophrenia have visual **hallucinations**—meaning they see things that are not there. But more common are **auditory** hallucinations—meaning they hear things that are not there. Sometimes people with schizophrenia hear friendly voices. More often, the voices are harsh, critical, or frightening. It's also possible to have **olfactory** hallucinations of bad or strange smells. There are also **tactile** hallucinations. For example, someone might feel certain that bugs are crawling on his skin.

Opposite: Paranoia, which is the belief that other people are watching you or somehow plotting against you, is very common among people with schizophrenia.

Thought Disorders. Sometimes it's hard to understand people with schizophrenia because when they speak, their words can come out in the wrong order. This is called "disorganized speech." Sometimes this can become so severe that words are randomly strung together; this is called "word salad." Or sometimes they have trouble making their thoughts connect to one another in a logical way. People with thought disorders might invent many new words that don't make sense, or they might stop talking

SOME TYPES OF DELUSIONS

- *Grandiose.* Believing you have magical or extraordinary abilities. A person may believe that he has been chosen by God to save the world.
- *Identification.* Believing you are a well-known historical or current figure, such as Christopher Columbus or a movie star.
- *Persecution.* Thinking that other people want to harm you. A person might believe the government is putting chemicals into the water to poison her.
- *Reference.* Thinking that world events and the behaviors of other people somehow relate to you. A person might assume that strangers laughing in a restaurant are making fun of him.
- *Sin or guilt.* Believing you are responsible for tragedies that take place. For instance, a person might feel guilty because she thinks she caused a plane crash.
- *Thought broadcasting.* Thinking that you can send your thoughts into other people's minds. For example, a person might believe she can control other people around her by sending them mental commands.
- *Thought insertion.* Believing that other people are putting thoughts into your mind. For instance, a person may believe that terrorists are using radio signals to control him.

RULING THINGS OUT

It is important to remember that any of the symptoms we've mentioned could be caused by something other than schizophrenia. For example, the disease called epilepsy can have some similar symptoms. So can some brain tumors. A severe viral infection could cause hallucinations. Even a vitamin deficiency called pellagra could cause some of these symptoms. It is important to have a full exam by a doctor before jumping to any conclusions.

right in the middle of a sentence, which is called "thought blocking." Some people with this symptom can't stop speaking in rhyme; this is called "clanging."

Negative Symptoms

Some things that are easy for healthy people, people with schizophrenia find difficult or impossible. Those are called negative symptoms. Again, that doesn't mean good or bad. It just means that something you expect to see in a healthy person is missing from the person with schizophrenia. Negative symptoms include:

- *Flat affect.* Someone with a flat affect does not show emotion in her face or voice. She speaks in a monotone way.
- *Lack of conversation.* People with schizophrenia are sometimes unwilling or unable to talk with others.
- *Lack of motivation.* People with this symptom can't get interested in or excited about anything.

A common trait of people with schizophrenia is flat affect, which means they sometimes don't show emotion in their faces or voices.

Making a Diagnosis

Only a doctor can say for sure if a person has schizophrenia. To figure it out, doctors use something called the *Diagnostic and Statistical Manual of Mental Disorders* (*DSM*). The manual defines all the disorders and gives instructions about how to diagnose patients. The *DSM* was updated for the fifth time in 2013, so people usually refer to the *DSM-5* (the number five refers to the fifth edition of the book).

CASE STUDY: PATTI

Patti was a good kid. She did well at school, had plenty of friends, and got along well with her brother. But after Patti graduated from high school, problems began. She took classes at the local community college, but she soon lost interest. She had trouble getting out of bed in the morning.

One evening, she threw a plate of food across the room, cursed loudly, and then ran outside. She shouted at her parents, "You will never take me alive!"

Patti's symptoms just got worse. One day she locked herself in her bedroom and screamed for hours. When at last her father broke down the door, Patti was sitting on the floor, rocking back and forth.

Her parents took her to the hospital. She told the doctor that she was being watched by "secret forces" who put thoughts in her head. The doctor gave her a drug called risperidone, which calmed her. In a few weeks, the drug began to work and her symptoms went away. She was able to return to college.

According to the *DSM-5*, schizophrenia happens along a **spectrum**. This means that there are different varieties of the disorder, and that some are more intense than others. For example, a person can have what's called *schizophreniform disorder*, which is like schizophrenia but doesn't last as long. Another type is called *schizoaffective disorder*, which is when a person has some symptoms of schizophrenia and also a mood disorder, such as depression.

Additional Symptoms

There are a few other symptoms of schizophrenia that aren't described as either positive or negative.

According to the Department of Health and Human Services, as many as 200,000 homeless people may be suffering from schizophrenia. If that estimate is correct, that would be nearly one-third of the US homeless population.

Grossly Disorganized Behavior. This is a term for behavior that does not seem appropriate to the particular situation. For instance, a person with this symptom might suddenly become upset for no reason. Or she might act extremely silly for reasons no one else can understand. Dressing in a very odd manner—wearing a swimsuit in the snow, for example—could also be considered grossly disorganized behavior.

Emotional Disturbances. As we mentioned earlier, people with schizophrenia may not express much emotion. This is called a "flat affect."

The emotions of people with schizophrenia can also change suddenly and without warning. People with schizophrenia often respond to internal voices or to their own thoughts rather than the real world around them. That's why they might laugh out loud or start crying—seemingly out of nowhere.

Text-Dependent Questions

1. What is the difference between a positive and negative symptom?
2. Name some positive symptoms of schizophrenia.
3. Name some negative symptoms.
4. What are some types of schizophrenia?

Research Project

Some famous people from history have had schizophrenia. For example, author Jack Keroac, ballet dancer Vaclav Nijinsky, First Lady Mary Todd Lincoln, football player Lionel Aldridge, jazz musician Buddy Bolden, Syd Barrett of the rock group Pink Floyd, and award-winning mathematician John Nash may all have had some form of schizophrenia. Choose a person who interests you and write a brief biography, focusing on how the disorder influenced his or her life.

CHAPTER FOUR

TREATMENT OF SCHIZOPHRENIA

Words to Understand

antipsychotics: drugs used to treat schizophrenia and certain other extreme mental disorders.

noncompliance: refusing to follow rules or do as instructed.

psychosocial: the interaction between someone's thoughts and the outside world of relationships.

Schizophrenia is a confusing disease—for doctors, patients, and for the patients' families and friends. It can be frightening to feel so out of sync with the rest of the world. It can also be frightening to see someone you love struggle with this disorder.

The good news is that there are a number of treatments that can help people manage their disorder and have good lives. Dr. Torrey, who was mentioned in an earlier chapter, wrote, "I have seen patients with virtually every [symptom] go on to almost complete recovery."

Types of Medicine

With many disorders, there is disagreement about whether drugs are necessary. For example, someone who is depressed

People with schizophrenia almost always need to be on some form of medication. Medical practitioners will explain how and when to take the medicine.

might or might not need to take medicine. Different doctors might give different advice. But with schizophrenia, there is almost no disagreement. Medication is by far the best and most important treatment. The use of psychiatric drugs reduces symptoms, shortens the amount of time spent in the hospital, and lowers the likelihood of more problems in the future.

Of course, not all drugs work for all people. And they do not work well on all symptoms. Medication is most effective for positive symptoms—delusions, hallucinations, and thought disorders.

The medicines used to treat schizophrenia are called **antipsychotics**. There are two types, "typical" and "atypical." These words refer to when the drugs were first used. Typical

CASE STUDY: JOHN

From a young age, John was different. He had very little interest in other children. He only wanted to play alone with his toy airplanes and cars. Teachers disliked John and even called him "backward." But John's parents encouraged him to read and let him perform science experiments at home.

John attended college and became a professor, but his odd ways kept him apart from most people. Over time, his symptoms got worse. John began to believe that the newspaper contained messages from aliens. He had to be hospitalized often, and his family suffered.

But this did not stop John, whose full name was John Nash, from becoming one of the most brilliant mathematicians the world has known. He won many awards, including a Nobel Prize in 1994. His story was made into the film *A Beautiful Mind*.

antipsychotics were first used in the late 1950s. Atypical antipsychotics are more recent, and they work on the brain in a slightly different way.

Typical Antipsychotics

These drugs have names like haloperidol, fluphenazine, and chlorpromazine (see table on page 36). They block the brain's access to dopamine, that chemical discussed in an earlier chapter. Less dopamine in the brain can reduce the symptoms of schizophrenia.

However, as also mentioned earlier, a drop in dopamine can *cause* other symptoms. The side effects of typical antipsychotics can look very much like new symptoms. The experience can be very unpleasant at times. Side effects

Sometimes, a person with schizophrenia may need to be hospitalized in order to keep him from hurting himself or others.

ANTIPSYCHOTIC DRUGS

Medicines usually have two names. One is the official (or "generic") name and the other is a sort of nickname given to the drug by the company that sells it. Often these nicknames (or "brand names") are easier to pronounce and remember than

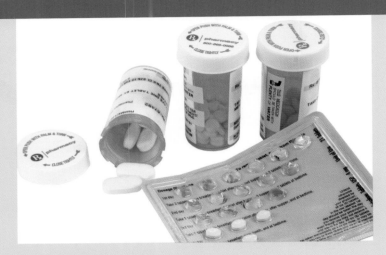

the generic names. But the drug is the same, no matter what you call it. Here are some generic and brand names for different antipsychotic drugs.

Generic Name	Brand Name
Typical Antipsychotics	
haloperidol	Haldol
fluphenazine HCl	Prolixin
trifluoperazine HCl	Stelazine
thiothixene hcl	Navane
perphenazine	Trilafon
chlorpromazine	Thorazine
thioridazine	Mellaril
Atypical Antipsychotics	
clozapine	Clozaril
risperidone	Risperdal
olanzapine	Zyprexa
quetiapine fumarate	Seroquel
ziprasidone hcl	Geodon
Iloperidone	Fanapt

include extreme tiredness, facial tics, tremors, restlessness, weight gain, and seizures.

Typical antipsychotic drugs can work very well, but many patients do *not* like taking them. Refusing to take medicine is called **noncompliance**. Rates of noncompliance for typical antipsychotics can be as high as 40 percent. This can result in these persons having to be hospitalized so that they don't hurt themselves or others.

However, not only do typical antipsychotics work well on symptoms, they can actually slow the disease down. So it is very important that patients follow their doctor's advice. People respond differently to different medications. So it can take time to figure out what drug is best for a specific patient.

DID YOU KNOW?

There are many medications that treat schizophrenia. It can take time to find the one that works best for a particular patient.

Atypical Antipsychotics

Atypical antipsychotics were first used in the United States in the 1990s. These drugs also block dopamine, but less strongly than the typical antipsychotic drugs. They also block serotonin, another substance mentioned earlier. This might be why the drugs do a good job of treating the symptoms of schizophrenia without so many side effects.

Unfortunately, these drugs do still have some side effects. For example, clozapine can cause a blood disorder that can be fatal. It only happens in about 1 percent of people who take the drug, but it is very serious. People on clozapine need to have regular blood tests.

Psychiatric drugs don't just affect the brain—they affect the entire body. This means they can cause side effects; people taking antipsychotics usually need regular check ups.

Other atypical antipsychotics can cause eye problems, heart problems, and seizures. Most of them cause weight gain. However, there are other drugs that can be used to counteract some or all of these issues.

Other Treatments

As we said, antipsychotic drugs are almost always the first choice for treatment. But there are other therapies that can help people with schizophrenia. These are called **psychosocial** treatments. They affect not only the mind but also the way the person relates to the world. Usually, these treatments are used along with the medicine being used.

When treating people on the schizophrenia spectrum, therapists focus on practical things. A therapist might help a patient practice her social skills. Group therapy, where people with schizophrenia talk to and comfort each other, is becoming more popular. Therapists might also help a patient to think of ways to manage hallucinations, such as listening to music to drown out voices.

Sometimes it is helpful to bring family members into therapy. It can be very stressful to be a family member of someone with schizophrenia, and talking can be helpful. A lot depends on the specific situation. As discussed earlier, families do not cause schizophrenia. But they can play an important role in recovery.

Group and family therapy can help people with schizophrenia deal with the pressures of daily life.

RELAPSE PREVENTION

When someone is ill, gets better, and then gets ill again, that is called a *relapse*. Doctors often work with schizophrenics on relapse prevention. This might include educating a patient and his family about sleep habits, stress management, and remembering to take medications. In addition, most therapists will help patients and their families come up with a "safety plan." It is a good idea to have planned in advance for what should happen if the family member with schizophrenia has a relapse.

Helping Someone with Schizophrenia

It is very difficult to have a close friend or family member who struggles with schizophrenia. Experts suggest a few things you can do.

Support their treatment. Sometimes, people with schizophrenia do not want to take drugs or continue with therapy. This is easy to understand: As mentioned already, antipsychotic drugs can feel very unpleasant. But it is very important that people with the disorder follow the treatment they have been given. They need the encouragement of their families and friends.

Respond carefully to delusions. When someone with schizophrenia tells you about a delusion, it can be hard to know what to say. The best approach is to neither agree nor disagree with the person. Don't tell the person he is wrong. If he believes that aliens poisoned the water, you have no chance of convincing him otherwise. You will probably just

Opposite: Families need to be involved in their loved ones' treatments.

upset him. Instead, you might say, "Actually I don't see things that way, but I understand that you do." Then try to move the conversation to other topics where you can both agree.

Take care of yourself, too. Remember that the person you love has a very serious illness. It's natural to feel angry or sad about the situation. Don't be afraid to ask for help from others. Talking to someone else about your feelings might help you be more patient and understanding with your family member or friend.

Text-Dependent Questions

1. What are the two main types of drugs used to treat schizophrenia?
2. What is the difference between generic and brand-name drugs?
3. What are the side effects of antipsychotic drugs?
4. What else can be done to help schizophrenics, in addition to medication?

Research Project

Compare and contrast the treatment of schizophrenia with another disorder, like anxiety or depression. What are the treatment options for each type of disorder? What is similar about the treatments? Why do you think some of the treatments differ?

Further Reading

BOOKS

Iorizzo, Carrie. *Schizophrenia and Psychotic Disorders.* New York: Crabtree, 2014.

Friedman, Michelle S. *Everything You Need to Know About Schizophrenia.* New York: Rosen, 2000.

Sacks, Elyn R. *The Center Cannot Hold: My Journey through Madness.* New York: Hyperion, 2007.

Torrey, E. Fuller. *Surviving Schizophrenia: A Family Manual.* New York: HarperCollins, 2013.

ONLINE

American Academy of Childhood and Adolescent Psychiatry. "Facts for Families: Schizophrenia in Children." www.aacap.org/App_Themes/AACAP/docs/facts_for_families/49_schizophrenia_in_children.pdf.

National Alliance on Mental Illness. "What is Schizophrenia?" www.nami.org/Template.cfm?Section=schizophrenia9.

National Institute of Mental Health. "Schizophrenia." nimh.nih.gov/health/topics/schizophrenia/index.shtml.

Schizophrenia and Related Disorders Alliance of America. www.sardaa.org/.

Schizophrenia.com. www.schizophrenia.com.

LOSING HOPE?

This free, confidential phone number will connect you to counselors who can help.

National Suicide Prevention Lifeline

1-800-273-TALK (1-800-273-8255)

"Mental illness is nothing to be ashamed of, but stigma and bias shame us all. Together, we will replace stigma with acceptance, ignorance with understanding, fear with new hope for the future. Together, we will build a stronger nation for the new century, leaving no one behind."
—Bill Clinton

Series Glossary

acute: happening powerfully for a short period of time.

affect: as a noun, the way someone seems on the outside—including attitude, emotion, and voice (pronounced with the emphasis on the first syllable, "AFF-eckt").

atypical: different from what is usually expected.

bipolar: involving two, opposite ends.

chronic: happening again and again over a long period of time.

comorbidity: two or more illnesses appearing at the same time.

correlation: a relationship or connection.

delusion: a false belief with no connection to reality.

dementia: a mental disorder, featuring severe memory loss.

denial: refusal to admit that there is a problem.

depressant: a substance that slows down bodily functions.

depression: a feeling of hopelessness and lack of energy.

deprivation: a hurtful lack of something important.

diagnose: to identify a problem.

empathy: understanding someone else's situation and feelings.

epidemic: a widespread illness.

euphoria: a feeling of extreme, even overwhelming, happiness.

hallucination: something a person sees or hears that is not really there.

heredity: the passing of a trait from parents to children.

hormone: a substance in the body that helps it function properly.

hypnotic: a type of drug that causes sleep.

impulsivity: the tendency to act without thinking.

inattention: distraction; not paying attention.

insomnia: inability to fall asleep and/or stay asleep.

licensed: having an official document proving one is capable with a certain set of skills.

manic: a high level of excitement or energy.

misdiagnose: to incorrectly identify a problem.

moderation: limited in amount, not extreme.

noncompliance: refusing to follow rules or do as instructed.

onset: the beginning of something; pronounced like "on" and "set."

outpatient: medical care that happens while a patient continues to live at home.

overdiagnose: to determine more people have a certain illness than actually do.

pediatricians: doctors who treat children and young adults.

perception: awareness or understanding of reality.

practitioner: a person who actively participates in a particular field.

predisposition: to be more likely to do something, either due to your personality or biology.

psychiatric: having to do with mental illness.

psychiatrist: a medical doctor who specializes in mental disorders.

psychoactive: something that has an effect on the mind and behavior.

psychosis: a severe mental disorder where the person loses touch with reality.

psychosocial: the interaction between someone's thoughts and the outside world of relationships.

psychotherapy: treatment for mental disorders.

relapse: getting worse after a period of getting better.

spectrum: a range; in medicine, from less extreme to more extreme.

stereotype: a simplified idea about a type of person, not connected to actual individuals.

stimulant: a substance that speeds up bodily functions.

therapy: treatment of a problem; can be done with medicine or simply by talking with a therapist.

trigger: something that causes something else.

Index

Page numbers in *italics* refer to photographs.

About the Author

H. W. POOLE is a writer and editor of books for young people, such as the *Horrors of History* series (Charlesbridge). She is also responsible for many critically acclaimed reference books, including *Political Handbook of the World* (CQ Press) and the *Encyclopedia of Terrorism* (SAGE). She was coauthor and editor of the *History of the Internet* (ABC-CLIO), which won the 2000 American Library Association RUSA award.

About the Advisor

ANNE S. WALTERS is Clinical Associate Professor of Psychiatry and Human Behavior. She is the Clinical Director of the Children's Partial Hospital Program at Bradley Hospital, a program that provides partial hospital level of care for children ages 7–12 and their families. She also serves as Chief Psychologist for Bradley Hospital. She is actively involved in teaching activities within the Clinical Psychology Training Programs of the Alpert Medical School of Brown University and serves as Child Track Seminar Co-Coordinator. Dr. Walters completed her undergraduate work at Duke University, graduate school at Georgia State University, internship at UTexas Health Science Center, and postdoctoral fellowship at Brown University. Her interests lie in the area of program development, treatment of severe psychiatric disorders in children, and psychotic spectrum disorders.

Photo Credits

Photos are for illustrative purposes only; individuals depicted in the photos, both on the cover and throughout this book, are only models.

Cover Photo: Shutterstock/Karuka

Dollar Photo Club: 10 jorisvo; 11 Stefanos Kyriazis; 13 fasphotographic; 14 Burlingham; 18 elenarostunova; 20 Monkey Business; 25 Alex Bramwell; 28 SerglyN; 30 Giuseppe Porzani; 33 Burlingham; 36 Jaimie Duplass; 38 Phase4Photography; 41 Monkey Business. **iStock.com:** 35 Tomwang112; 39 Alina555. **Wikimedia Commons:** 17 Ferdinand Schmutzer.